BRITTANY LAMB

Stuck at Twelve

How One Man's Decision to Drink and Drive Changed My Life

First published by Think Fifty Twenty 2021

Copyright © 2021 by Brittany Lamb

All rights reserved. No part of this publication may be reproduced, stored or transmitted in any form or by any means, electronic, mechanical, photocopying, recording, scanning, or otherwise without written permission from the publisher. It is illegal to copy this book, post it to a website, or distribute it by any other means without permission.

Designations used by companies to distinguish their products are often claimed as trademarks. All brand names and product names used in this book and on its cover are trade names, service marks, trademarks and registered trademarks of their respective owners. The publishers and the book are not associated with any product or vendor mentioned in this book. None of the companies referenced within the book have endorsed the book.

First edition

ISBN: 979-8-9853614-0-7

This book was professionally typeset on Reedsy.
Find out more at reedsy.com

Preface

Stories are often told **about** people, and not **by** the people who own the story. I am taking control of my narrative and telling my story, in my own words.

This is my life, the story that I have lived. Some of it, at least. The main focus is on the car crash that I allowed to dictate my life for years. My story is based on my experiences and my memories, with a little help from my siblings, newspaper articles, and a lot of help from my therapist. I wouldn't have remembered a lot of what happened when I was 12 and I would not have had the tools and confidence to learn and grow from these experiences had I not gone into therapy.

I decided to write this story because I have kept so much inside for so long. When I started talking on Victim Impact Panels about my car crash with MADD (Mother's Against Drunk Driving), I realized that there are so many others who have been through a trauma, whether it was similar to mine (drinking and driving crash), or different. I want to help bring trauma out in the open, and to help others realize that it is okay to talk about what has happened to them or around them.

My hope is that you get something out of reading this, whether it changes your viewpoint on therapy, stops you from drinking and driving, or allows you to realize that other people have trauma too and you are not alone. I hope your eyes can be opened to how your actions can affect others in unimaginable ways.

I am not perfect. I am far from it. Same with this book. But I wrote it and

I am proud that I did it. I am proud of who I am and how I have overcome obstacles in my life. I will no longer be a victim of my circumstances. Writing out the events of my life have allowed me to see how much I have grown and will continue to grow and learn from what has happened. I hope to help others learn and grow from what has happened in their lives.

Be proud of who you are. Don't get stuck in a trauma or stuck in a situation – there is always a way out. You just need to be willing to look for it.

Acknowledgement

I had a lot of help and encouragement writing this book. A huge thank you goes out to Becky Lauridsen, who was the first person in twenty years to fully hear and understand my story, and to help me face it head on.

Thank you to Mary Overton, my long-time best friend who helped me through many times in my life and is always someone I can count on to be there for me. Mary helped edit as I wrote, which helped tremendously in keeping me motivated.

Thank you also to my sister-in-law, Amanda Lamb, and my beautiful friends Lexi Deckert and Kelley Klein for taking time out of their busy lives to edit and review everything you are about to read.

Thank you to my love, Ben Frenzen, for being my rock and keeping me sane and grounded. You tell me like it is, you help through the tough times, and are always there for me.

Thank you to my son Landon for being you - sweet, smart ,and loving. I hope you know how strong you are and how much you are loved.

Finally, thank you to my family for being there for me through everything. Your support, love, and humor always gets me through tough times, even if I refuse to talk about what I am going through. I love you Mom, Dad, Ryan, Jerome, and Kristin!

I

Part One

"You intended to harm me, but God intended it for good, to accomplish what is now being done the saving of many lives."
(Genesis 50:20)

1

The Beginning

I should have been on that helicopter. I should be dead. I shouldn't have to be going through this pain. How did I get here?

Everything is in slow motion. Headlights are coming right at me. I throw my arms up to shield my face. The impact hits us. Time stands still. The car spins. Another crash. Silence.

I wake up to the smell of blood with tears running down my face. This feeling is something I will never forget. I can still feel it sometimes when it's quiet and I'm thinking about the crash. It's haunting, but there is a reason I remember. I remember to keep my Aunt's spirit alive. I remember because I survived for a reason. I survived to tell my story, to help others, and to be a powerful force in this world.

December 14th, 1997

I got home from rehearsal at my dance studio and My Aunt Julie had surprised me with tickets to see the Nutcracker, performed by the Colorado Ballet in Denver. This was the first professional ballet I had ever seen and being a dancer in our studio's production of the Nutcracker, I was very excited to see it live! It was a Sunday night - a school night - but the show was early in the evening, and we would be home by 9:00 pm. I put on a pair of black pants, my favorite light purple sweater, and my favorite pair of shoes.

After saying goodbye to my parents, my Aunt Julie and I went out to her car. It was an older-model gold Volkswagen, with a khaki interior, dark brown dash, tape deck and green lighting. It faintly smelled of flowers, and were always an assortment of papers on the floor. I got in, moved the papers to the back, and put on my seat belt. My Aunt got in, and we started backing out. I asked about her seat belt; she told me it was broken. We turned down the road and headed off to the ballet.

We got to the theater and I was awestruck. It was bustling with people; there were Christmas lights strung across the performing arts center, and people were dressed in their finest winter coats and dresses. We made our way into the theater and settled in to our red velvet seats. We were on the first level and had a really great view of the stage - I felt like I was a part of the show.

If you haven't seen the Nutcracker, I highly recommend it. The costumes are one of a kind, the dancing is spectacular, the music is iconic. I kept a close eye on the character Herr Drosselmeyer because that is who I was playing in my studio's production. I remember being entranced by the Sugar Plum Fairy and her gorgeous dancing – and her turns on pointe. She was magnificent. I laughed when the kids came out of Mother Ginger's dress and wondered how I could be a part of such an experience.

After the show was over, Aunt Julie wanted to buy me something to remember the show by. There was a long line at the souvenir table, but we were in no hurry. It took me a long time to decide what to get when it was finally my turn to look. There were so many cute trinkets, ornaments, and t-shirts to choose from. I eventually decided on a t-shirt and a ballet ornament – a small pair of glass pointe ballet shoes, tied with a pink ribbon.

THE BEGINNING

The crowd had thinned out by this time, in fact, there were only a handful of people left in the lobby. We walked out to the car; it was chilly outside but I never liked wearing a jacket. We strolled back through the Buell Theater, taking in the Christmas sites once again through the open air. We got to the parking garage, and like the lobby in the theater, it was relatively empty. When I got in the car, I remember staring at a concrete wall that had graffiti painted along the top and I was trying to read what it said as we backed out of the spot. I put my seat belt on, placed my treasures in my lap, and Aunt Julie headed out of the garage.

We were blasting music while singing along to every song. The Spice Girls were my favorite band - and luckily, they were Aunt Julie's favorite too! In between singing, I remember commenting how lucky we were to be hitting every green light on Broadway. The lights were green for as far as I could see and there was hardly any traffic on the streets. I loved watching the lights turn from green to yellow to red, and then back to green, wondering to myself if we were going to have to stop or not. We never hit one red light.

Aunt Julie turned onto Santa Fe. Around the same time a man named Jerry was leaving a sports bar with his two friends. After spending a Sunday having a few beers, likely watching football, it was time for them to go home. I imagine Jerry picked them up earlier in the day and they went to the bar to have some nachos, knock back a few beers, talk about their girlfriends or jobs. They may have even taken a shot or two to celebrate their team's victory on that Sunday evening.

They had work in the morning and the games were over, so they paid the tab and headed home. I always wonder if it crossed Jerry's mind that he might not be okay to drive. Was this a habit to drink a few beers and then get behind the wheel? Not thinking he was intoxicated that night, Jerry and his friends got into his black two-door Mazda.

The Crash

My Aunt and I, still listening to Spice Girls, were about one mile from my parents' house when the black Mazda, driving northbound, crossed into the southbound lanes. It was estimated he was driving 50-60 mph on Santa Fe, which at the time was a construction zone with a speed limit of 40 mph. The only thing separating the north and southbound lanes of traffic were large, round, orange construction cones.

We never saw it coming.

Headlights shone in our eyes, and Aunt Julie threw her arm across me. I put my arms up in the air to block my face, and then the impact happened. It was the loudest noise I have ever heard in my life. Glass started showering me as the car was spinning in what seemed like a slow-motion action scene in a movie. There was another hit and then silence.

All I could hear was myself crying as I sat in the car, looking up at the night sky through the open windshield. I don't know how much time had passed before I heard the sirens. I looked over and saw my Aunt slumped over the steering wheel, blood covering the side of her face and matting her curly brown hair. She wasn't moving. I started screaming for her to wake up.

Still not knowing how much time had passed, I finally saw firefighters running toward the car. A face came to the open windshield - a firefighter. I noticed right away that he had a mustache and blue eyes. I would later learn that his name was Fred. I told him not to leave me.

Fred started pulling on the car door frame, trying to get the door open. It wouldn't budge. I was focused on getting out of the car and I lost track of what was happening on my Aunt Julie's side of the car. I was told not to move. Another firefighter came over with a heavy blanket. He said he was going

THE BEGINNING

to put this blanket over me, and there was going to be a lot of noise. But he promised to get me out of the car.

Everything went dark once he placed the blanket over my head and body. The blanket felt itchy on my hands and smelled like sawdust. It must have been made of wool. I could hear Fred talking near me, so I knew he hadn't left. There was a loud noise right above my head - it sounded like metal on metal, a grinding noise that you would hear in a mechanic's shop.

> **There are bright lights all around, people yelling, and I can feel an unusual heat in the air. It smells like gasoline and fire.**

I don't know how much time has passed, but the next thing I know, I am being lifted out of the car and my face and skin are exposed to the night air. I am lying on a stretcher and staring at the night sky, the cold air on my face. There are bright lights all around, people yelling, and I can feel an unusual heat in the air. It smells like gasoline and fire.

The stretcher is put into the ambulance and I find myself looking up at a white ceiling. There are people standing over me, talking about things I can't understand. An EMT has a pair of scissors, and he starts cutting my sweater. I fight against it, telling him this is my favorite sweater, and I am cold – please, please don't cut it off. I can't continue to fight back, though. I am too weak. I asked the firefighter, Fred, who had stayed by my side, to go get my t-shirt and ornament from the car that my Aunt bought me. And my shoes - I needed him to get my favorite shoes!

Fred stepped out of the ambulance. The doors were shut, and I heard the sirens turn on. The tubes and tools started swaying in the ambulance. I don't know how long we were in the ambulance, but suddenly I am being wheeled out into the cold air once again. We go into the emergency room, where the florescent lights shine in my eyes so I close them tight, listening to the voices above me.

I open my eyes and focus on one nurse's face. He had brown hair, brown eyes, a soft, round gentle face. He was wearing green scrubs. He asked me what my name was. I knew my name. I knew I could tell him. But I didn't. I couldn't find my voice. I was scared and confused. I didn't know exactly what had happened or where I was. I was all alone, even with a dozen doctors and nurses in the room.

* * *

I wake up in the ICU. There are machines all around me and tubes going in and out of my arms and throat. It is very dark and quiet except for the lights of the machines and the sound of a heart monitor. A nurse is standing behind me. She tells me that I was in a car crash, and I am about to go into another surgery. She also tells me to be strong and that I will be okay. I start trying to talk, and then realize that this tube in my throat won't let me. The nurse puts her hand on me and tells me to calm down. I close my eyes and I drift back to sleep.

* * *

Reflection

How do you define trauma? Not what the dictionary says or not what Google says, but what you believe it to be. There is no wrong answer here - everyone sees trauma differently.

THE BEGINNING

Have you ever had a traumatic experience? What do you remember of it? Do you wish you could remember more, or are you okay with blocking it out of memory?

2

Memories

My family is one of those close-knit, matching-pajama-wearing, annoyingly perfect families. Ha! Just kidding. We are far from perfect (and don't wear matching pajamas) - but we love each other, tell it like it is, and have a lot of fun. My parents were married in 1982 and are still together today. My older brother, Ryan, is 15 months older than I am; my younger brother, Jerome, is 4 years younger, and my little sister, Kristin, is 9 years younger.

Growing up, we had one of those big, old-school video cameras. I am so thankful that we had one. After the crash, I used to love popping the VHS into the player and re-watching memories that I couldn't remember. There was me in my Easter dress, probably 6 years old, playing in the park. I see my dad singing "Squeeze Box" by the Who to the camera, sitting in the black and gold rocking chair that was in our living room. There is video of my brothers and I playing with golden retriever puppies. I don't know if I would have these memories without that camera. I see the memories. I want to see more; I want to remember more, but I can't.

My memories come in waves, and there are times when I don't know if it's real or if I made it up. Traumatic brain injuries affect people in different ways. Due to where my head hit in the crash, my frontal lobe received the most damage. The frontal lobe controls several functions, such as expression of emotions, elements of your personality, reasoning, and coordination.

Long-term severity of damage to the frontal lobe depends on many factors, one of which is your age. I was 12 when the crash happened, and my brain was still developing. Below are some common side effects that I have experienced with my head injury:

- Quick behavior changes
- Mood changes/depression
- Memory loss
- Confusion
- Headaches
- Inability to understand or comprehend
- Impaired judgment

Full recovery can take months, years, or may never occur. Besides depression, I think my memory loss is what has affected me the most. Apart from the memories I get from watching the camera playback, I don't remember a lot of details about my childhood before the crash. However, there are a few moments that stand out. It's almost as if I can press play in my head and the memory rolls like it's on the camera.

The Principal's Office

I went to the principal's office once, in fifth grade. I snapped a girls' sports bra and had to go have a chat with the principal. I was mortified. I was the girl who never did anything wrong and always followed the rules. The problem with getting into trouble at school was that my dad worked in the administration office for the school district. He was well known in the schools (especially in our school). I was very embarrassed about having to go to the office; just thinking he would find out made me nervous that I would disappoint him.

Here I was, sitting in the principal's office with my friend who had told the teacher what I did. Who cares that she did it to me first, I didn't tell on her! Thinking back on the moment, I guess I was upset I got caught. Sitting there, I didn't say much or stand up for myself. I simply sat there in silence, just waiting for the moment to be over when we would get our punishment and be allowed to go back to class.

We were asked what happened and both told our stories. I believed the principal was an authority, and I was merely there to take my punishment. Well, the punishment didn't end up being much of anything. I think I missed a recess or two, and I don't know if my parents ever found out.

That experience made me more of a focused student - I hated the feeling of being in trouble, or of someone being mad at me. I tried to do everything right to please others, and to this day still see myself trying to make others happy, often to my detriment.

The Paint Can

I once had a can of paint thrown at me by my little brother Jerome. He was mad that my older brother, Ryan, and I weren't letting him play "Where's Mario" on Nintendo. My dad had a gallon of paint sitting by the front door for a job he was working on. Jerome picked it up and started swinging it by the handle like he was going to throw it at us if we didn't let him play.

On the third or fourth swing, the can slipped out of his hand and POP! Paint went everywhere. It seemed to have missed me and Ryan, but a huge glob of white paint sat seeping into the floor. Oh, and my parents had just put in new carpet.

We scattered. We all ran into my brother's room and hid under the bed. My dad is very even tempered. It takes a lot for him to get mad - usually, he just gets disappointed. We heard him run into the room, say a few expletives, run back to the kitchen to grab supplies and started cleaning it up. He didn't look for us or tell us to come clean it. We stayed under that bed for what seemed like hours, until we sheepishly crawled out to assess the damage. Dad was still in the living room scraping the white paint out of the carpet with a putty knife. He didn't say a word.

Despite the efforts of my dad to clean it up, remnants of white paint hardened, and we had a permanent piece of Jerome's artwork for years, until we put in hardwood floors.

Riding Bikes

There were a lot of kids in the neighborhood, and we rode our bikes together until dusk. I would ride with one girl down to the park, where we befriended the birds. We were carefree, running after the ducks and geese, feeding them with stale bread from our houses, and picking them up like they were our pets.

My brothers and I would take the dollars we got from visiting our Grandma and ride our bikes to 7-11. Cherry Slurpee's were my summertime staple. My dad's office was a mile from the house, so we would stop on the way to say hello or bring him some candy on our way back. We parked our bikes by the door in the back, waving to the security cameras. Someone would always hear or see us, and let us in.

The office smelled like new carpet all the time. We drew on the whiteboard in the conference room and walked around saying hello to everyone we knew. We would stop by the cafeteria to see if there were any snacks sitting out on the tables. Then, we would hop back on our bikes and race each other the mile home, always trying to find a new shortcut. I'm sure I never won a race.

We were independent, exploring our neighborhood and being carefree kids. We wouldn't be in the house long on the weekends - just enough time to do our chores so we could get out and go have some fun.

Grandpa

My brothers and I loved hopping in my Grandpa's truck when he visited to go to the park and fish for crawdads. Our Grandpa taught us how to make a fishing pole out of a stick and some string, to which we would bait with a hot dog. We would stand on a wooden bridge over a shallow creek and try to catch each crawdad we saw.

Once we caught all the crawdads we could find, Grandpa would carry our bucket back to the pickup where we would jump in the back and ride home. We left the bucket in the shade of the tree in the front lawn until our parents came home so we could show them off.

We also loved going to my Grandpa and Grandma's house. The smell was distinct - there was always something cooking in the oven, and that smell mixed with cigarette smoke and flowers. The carpet was a seventies green, the tile in the kitchen was black with colored specks. There were always animals around - kittens my Grandma would find and nurse back to health, with the rescued Mastiff always at her heels. We would explore the garage, learning from my Grandpa, and then go down to the basement and find treasures that my mom and her siblings had when she was our age.

We felt very adventurous!

The Pool

On her days off, my mom would always take us to the pool. It never failed that the pool was packed with families. We would search for our best friends and set our towels up on the grass, slather on sunscreen as fast as we could, and jump in. We would play Marco Polo and work on our handstands and underwater flips. We followed each other to the top of the stairs of the slide, going down and then climbing out to go down the slide again and again.

As soon as we heard "adult swim" it was a race to get to the snack line - every kid trying not to run so as not to get yelled at by the lifeguard, but wanting to be first in line. The pool was always fun, until we had to leave. It never failed that we knew that look on mom's face when it was time to go. We would hide under water, in the deep end, or behind people. But as soon as that lifeguard called adult swim, we knew it was time. We would come home exhausted.

Block Parties and Parades

We grew up in a great neighborhood. There were a ton of kids, and my best friends lived just a block away. One of our favorite summer traditions was the annual block party. The street would be closed off, and the neighbors would all get together for food and games. We would eat and wait for the sun to go down before playing flashlight tag or capture the flag.

Block parties were always a sign that summer was winding down and we had to head back to school soon. The biggest sign that summer was over, though, was the Western Welcome Week parade. I was often in the parade, whether it was for my dance class or, later in life, the high school dance team. I loved walking down the streets, waving and performing. After the parade was over, we would browse the craft booths, eat from the food vendors and swelter in the sun until we were sunburned and ready to go home.

***

My brothers, sister, and I had a happy childhood. It was full of memories and laughter. We were never grounded or got in big trouble. My parents worked hard. My mom worked nights so she could take care of us during the day, and my dad worked at the school district and also ran his own business. They worked hard so we could have a good life, and a good life is what we had. I don't want to say everything changed after the crash, but it was different.

***

Reflection

What is your earliest childhood memory?

What is your favorite childhood memory?

3

Ten Days

I clearly remember two nurses standing above me in the ICU. I don't remember their exact words, but I recall they told me they were going to get the tube out that was helping me breathe. Trying to describe the feeling of having the tube pulled out… makes me lost for words. It was like throwing up a footlong hot dog that hadn't been chewed, and when it was finally out, trying not to panic when you take your first breath on your own.

> **My parents come into the room and are standing over me. They tell me I was in a car crash, and I am okay. That is what people kept saying to me -** *I was going to be okay.*

The next memory I have is waking up in a hospital room. My older brother is sitting on the edge of the hospital bed, and the TV is on. The Denver Broncos are playing the San Diego Chargers and the Broncos are winning 24-3. That means it's a Sunday. The crash happened seven days ago. Ryan, my older brother, turns around and smiles at me. My parents come into the room and are standing over me. They tell me I was in a car crash, and I am okay. That is what people kept saying to me - *I was going to be okay.*

I also learned that my Aunt Julie had died on impact. I remember my dad telling me the news, with tears in his eyes and my mom standing next to him, her eyes red from crying. I had no memories of the crash at this time, and didn't understand the severity of it. I was just trying to comprehend everything that was going on around me. The machines, the doctors coming in and out, the words people were whispering. All I wanted to do was sleep and wake up to a different reality.

Physically, I was a mess. My face had hit the dashboard, resulting in a traumatic brain injury. The skin on my forehead had been torn and the bone exposed. There were shards of glass and pieces of dirt in my head. I had to be put in an induced coma to relieve the pressure on my brain.

My nose and cheekbones were crushed, and the top of my mouth had been fractured. I had gotten a hundred stitches in my forehead. I underwent hours of surgery to fix my nose and insert permanent mesh plates on the top of my mouth and in my cheekbones.

I had a broken collarbone and a few broken fingers. My left foot was broken. I had bruises where my seat belt had been, across my lap and chest. Those were the physical damages I had sustained within seconds of the crash. I had always thought I was lucky that it wasn't worse, because it very well could have been. These physical damages would heal quickly, even if I thought they never would. It was the mental distress that would take years upon years to heal - and will never heal completely.

Life in the Hospital

There were purple monkeys on the walls in the hospital room. I would stare at them as the doctors and nurses poked and prodded at me. I imagined myself being in a jungle, swinging through the trees and running away from everything. I thought of riding on the back of a cheetah, running into the sunset, escaping from everything. Then I would look out the window and it would be snowing, and that would bring me back to my reality.

It always seemed to be gloomy outside. I can still see the snowflakes swirling in the wind and landing on the roof outside my window. In contrast to the gloom outside, the flowers, cards, and stuffed animals that lined the windowsill and shelves brightened my room. I don't remember a lot of visitors, but I am sure I had them. I remember my older brother being there a lot, just sitting with me watching TV, while the nurses and doctors came in and out, checking my vitals and asking me about my pain.

One night, my dad's sister, my Aunt Ginny, was staying with me so that my parents could sleep in their own bed for the night. She was laying on the couch that was in the room. I had a nightmare that one of those purple monkeys came alive and attacked me. In the nightmare, the monkey called out to the spiders of the jungle and they started crawling down the soft cast on my arm. I woke up, trying to pull the tubes out of my arms and take off my cast. My Aunt Ginny ran to my bedside, calling for the nurses to come help. This was often how my trauma felt – a bad dream that was my reality.

While I was in the hospital, I received a personal performance from the Colorado Ballet. They heard what had happened because the crash was all over the news. I was sat in a wheelchair and was wheeled down into a hospital conference room. It was cold, but I had a heated blanket over my legs and the cool air from the hospital hallway felt fresh on my face.

There were about 10 dancers dressed in their costumes from the ballet company. They gave me a beautiful bouquet of flowers and a mini-Christmas tree filled with ballet themed ornaments. The soldiers pressed play on a boom box and the Sugar Plum Fairy danced across the room. It was a magical moment in an otherwise dismal time.

After the Colorado Ballet performance, I received a surprise visit from

Colorado Avalanche players Claude Lemieux, Patrick Roy, and Joe Sakic. They walked into the room with a basket of signed memorabilia and jerseys. They were larger than life. Not only was my Aunt Julie a huge Colorado Avalanche fan, but I was also such a fan that I had a gray and white cat named Lemieux! I don't know how the word got out that my cat was named after Claude Lemieux, but their visit helped put a smile on my face.

Getting Out

It was Christmas Eve morning, and the weather was cloudy and gray. I had two doctors visit me that morning. While one suggested I transfer to Children's Hospital, I had another doctor give me the all-clear to go home. Luckily, my parents agreed that I should leave the hospital. That was only ten days after the crash, and the doctor felt that I would heal faster if I was home. Plus - it was Christmas Eve! I needed to be home in my own bed.

The nurses came in and gave my parents discharge instructions. They set me up with a physical therapist to come to the house and start my therapy. Then, the nurses who had been so kind and caring during my visit started taking monitors off me. They rolled me to my side so they could take the tube out of my lower back.

The nurses helped me put on pajamas – light blue Winnie the Pooh pants and a button up long sleeve shirt. I had the brown hospital socks replaced with warm fuzzy socks. It felt so good to finally be out of a hospital gown and into my own clothes from home. I was wheeled out of the hospital with my doctors and nurses saying their goodbyes on the way out.

When we got outside, I saw that my dad had pulled the minivan up to the curb and I had a sinking feeling getting in. The last time I was in a car, I had ended up injured, my Aunt Julie ended up dying, and I spent ten days in the hospital. What would happen this time? I saw how excited my brothers were that I was going home, and I got into the car with help from my dad. I stared out the window the whole time, taking in a world that didn't pause for me while I was in the hospital. People were living their lives as usual and mine felt like it was just beginning again.

Guardian Angel

It wasn't until a few years later that I found out details of the crash. My parents kept newspaper articles in a basket that explained what had happened. While my family did not talk directly about the crash with me, mainly because I refused to talk or listen, I would eventually learn that Aunt Julie had died on impact. The car hit her side directly. There were three other cars involved, in addition to the Mazda and my Aunt's Volkswagen, and each of those drivers suffered minor injuries.

Once on scene, the firefighters were working hard to get me out of the car, and they realized that the jaws of life would be needed to open my car door. This would delay the AirLife helicopter from taking off, and even though my injuries were the most severe, they decided to let AirLife take the drunk driver who caused the crash into the helicopter to try to save his life.

The pilot was a Veteran with many years experience flying helicopters. Shortly after liftoff, the helicopter's blades became snagged in low-hanging power lines and the helicopter crashed to the fairway on a nearby golf course. There was an explosion, and everyone on board died. On board were Pete Abplanalp, Beth Barber, and Leslie Feldmann – all members of the Airlife Crew. Their lives ended while doing what they loved to do – helping others.

I survived because my car door was stuck. I thank the heavens that my door was unable to be opened by the strong hands of the firefighters. I truly believe that my Aunt Julie didn't leave the scene after she passed but stayed to ensure that I was okay. I imagine her holding that car door so tight that it wouldn't open. I imagine her using every last ounce of strength in her to ensure that I was going to be okay. She was at that moment, and still is today, my guardian angel.

* * *

This crash set me up for failure in the months and years to come. As a 12-year-old, I couldn't comprehend the *why* or the *what* that was happening to me. I didn't cope well with the special treatment I was getting - I hated feeling "special." I began to internalize everything - from the way I felt about the crash, to the way I felt about what was for dinner, to my opinion on basically everything. I didn't want to be a bother to anyone, and I didn't want to speak up - I might cause more problems.

All I thought about was going back to life before the crash. Back to my 12th birthday; starting the year over. If I pretended that nothing happened, then nothing would change. That's what I kept telling myself.

These events were unplanned and unwanted, but they happened. It was important to acknowledge what had happened. I know that there are forces at work more powerful than me, and life's events are a clear indication that I am not in charge. Whether you believe in a higher power, in luck, or anything else, what happens to you today does not have to determine how you see tomorrow. What happened to you in your past does not determine your future.

> **If I pretended that nothing happened, then nothing would change. That's what I kept telling myself.**

I wish I would have realized this as I headed back to finish 6th grade.

*　*　*

Reflection

Do you blame yourself for something that you know deep down was not your fault?

What are you internalizing that is holding you back from living up to your true potential?

Do you need to acknowledge a trauma? If so, what is holding you back?

4

My New Life

Middle school is a tough time. A lot of mental and physical growth are happening, kids are gaining a little more freedom, finding out who they are, and on top of all that they have to navigate puberty. I was four months into navigating this new world when the crash happened. The Friday before, our class had held a geography bee. I was going to be in the finals on Monday. It turned out that Monday looked a little different for me than I had imagined it was going to be.

Middle School

I went back to school a few weeks after the other kids returned from Christmas break. It was now February, and in Colorado February is dreary - everyone is itching for spring. I had a walking cast on my foot and my scars were fresh; they were very red and very noticeable. It hurt to write because I had suffered trauma to my right hand. The doctor had put pins in the fingers that I had broken, and I was still going through physical therapy to get my strength back. I was treated special - and I hated it. It took me longer to do things, it hurt to think, and I couldn't concentrate.

In sixth grade, I didn't feel bullied; I attribute that to kids feeling sorry for me and avoiding me. It almost felt like if they talked to me, something would happen to them. It was pathetic. The first instance of bullying I encountered was outside of school when my mom and I went to see a movie. We had a temporary handicap parking pass because of my broken foot and inability to walk far. I was on crutches at this time. A group of teenage boys were walking into the theater and had the nerve to make a comment about how "she's not handicapped." I was mortified. Luckily, my mom put them in their place and they ran the other way.

> **I was "that girl who got into the car crash." You have no idea how much I didn't want to be "that girl."**

Seventh and eighth grade came, and I was trying so hard to be normal. I still had trouble concentrating, and my headaches were constant. Food tasted different - and contributed to my headaches. I was quiet; quieter than I had ever been before. I lost a lot of friends over the summer between 6th and 7th grade because I stopped calling them. I felt that people only wanted to hang out with me because they felt sorry for me.

I came to school in the fall, and it was like I didn't exist to some people. I was "that girl who got into the car crash." You have no idea how much I didn't want to be "that girl."

Scarface

I remember the exact location the day I was first called Scarface. I was in 7th grade when it happened. The lockers were light blue, the hallway floor was light green. I was very familiar with the floor, as I spent a lot of time looking down. There were windows above the lockers, and I knew it was a cloudy day because the hallway was darker than usual.

I was wearing a long black skirt and a t-shirt - my hair was up in a bun because I had dance class after school. He was walking toward me, wearing an over-sized black t-shirt and over-sized jeans (JNCO's for those of us who grew up in the late 90's). His light, long blonde hair swept over his eyes, and he was a lot shorter than me. He usually called me Olive Oil, after the character in the old cartoon Popeye the Sailor Man, because I always wore my hair in a bun and was tall and thin. It didn't bother me, because I liked that cartoon and I thought it was a flirty joke.

As he passed me, he called me Scarface. SCARFACE.

My heart sank into my stomach and I ran into the bathroom and cried. I felt like my world was caving in. Did he really call me that, or was I imagining it? How could someone be so cruel? Did I have something to do with him calling me that, because I allowed him to call me Olive Oil? The nickname seemed to stick. Day after day, I would hear someone call me Scarface. I eventually became numb to it, acting like it didn't bother me, but I also started dreading going to school.

> **I was really good at putting on a brave face. Isn't that how a lot of us face adversity? Pretend it isn't happening and put on a brave face?**

Honestly, I have very few memories of middle school. I feel that I blocked out most of the bad memories and kept the positive ones. I remember my two best friends in middle school - Rachel and Kara. I have a lot of memories with these two girls: We were in the school play together where I was a dancer; we rode bikes together and had sleepovers; all three of us were in choir; we were sitting at the same table when we heard about Columbine; Rachel's mom would make us pancakes with homemade syrup when we slept over.

I was really good at putting on a brave face. Isn't that how a lot of us face adversity? Pretend it isn't happening and put on a brave face? I retreated into myself. I didn't speak up in class; I was mortified when a teacher called on me, even if I knew the answer. I didn't want to speak up because that would draw attention to me. Drawing attention to myself would mean people would look at me. Looking at me would mean they would see my scars. My scars meant trauma and pain for a lot of people. I was ashamed of them.

My First Time in Therapy

A few months after the crash I was taken to a therapist. I didn't speak to him. I was completely shut down and unwilling to see how talking about the trauma would help me. I was only 12, and thought it was a terrible idea to talk to someone about what had happened. I remember sitting in the front seat of my mom's car. It was a cloudy day. All the days seemed cloudy now. I didn't want to get out of the car. I don't know what she said or how she got me to go in, but I eventually gave up and followed her inside.

We went into the building that smelled of a doctor's office – clean, cold - and into the therapist's office. There was a large clock on the wall. The seats were brown leather - cold on my arms through my sweater. We sat with my mom for a bit, and they chatted. She then left the room – I was alone with the therapist. He would ask me questions; I would mostly shrug or say I don't know. We played scrabble. I didn't say anything.

During the second visit, we went for a walk along the trail behind the office building. I was a little more open this time, but we talked about trivial things, such as how school was going and what books I was reading. I never opened up enough to process anything substantial. That was the last time I saw a therapist until college.

High School

I went to high school expecting to be a different person. I told myself that this was an opportunity to meet new people and have new experiences. The problem was, though, that I hadn't changed myself. Nothing was going to change if I didn't change myself first. I wish I would have known that going in on the first day. I walked into my first class, sat down, turned to say hello to someone new, looked at them with wide eyes and turned back around without saying anything. I was the same person. It was just different scenery.

In high school, everyone is trying to find their own path. I didn't feel as bullied as I did in middle school; not that it didn't happen, but I wasn't made fun of to my face. I was shy, though. Painfully shy. That kind of shyness where you don't want to raise your hand in class, and you look down whenever you pass by someone.

It helped that I made the dance team, because I could be myself on the dance floor. We were also a tight group and I never felt pressured to be someone I wasn't. I was in track and field, too, and found a good group of people who didn't care about my scars or the fact that I was quieter than most people.

When I was with a large group, I would stick close to those people I was good friends with. I felt they understood me. I never said much when there was a group conversation. I didn't speak up or state my opinions, I just sat there quietly agreeing with whatever someone was saying or laughing at their jokes. I was trying to fit in just enough to make high school fun. I was jealous of those people who made it look so easy to make new friends. I would never be that person.

> **I always felt that I was stuck, mentally, in my 12-year-old mind. My world had stopped when the car crash happened, and I**

didn't know how to restart it.

I was good at hiding things in high school. I hid my insecurities when I needed to, and I hid behind the facade of being okay with who I was. I was a good student; I attended dances and parties and had crushes and my first kiss. I grew a lot in high school, but I still felt behind. I always felt that I was stuck, mentally, in my 12-year-old mind. My world had stopped when the car crash happened, and I didn't know how to restart it.

I had good friends in high school who understood me. The good souls who weren't judging me and who I could be myself around. We would sing in the car, laugh until it hurt, talk about our crushes. We would always have sleepovers and would go on road trips. Tiffany, Mary, and I buried a memory box. We would pile into my 4Runner to go to lunch. We would go out on the weekends, not really causing trouble but more than likely hanging out at Taco Bell or just sitting around someone's house. Mary. Tiffany. Stephanie. Kelly. Clasey. Amber. Katie. Some (not all) of the best people who helped me through high school.

I wanted to have more friends, be more outgoing, be able to hold a conversation with a stranger. It was like I was still a small child, hiding behind a smile and trying to figure out how to fit in with the big kids.

* * *

I felt like an iceberg. People saw me, saw that I had scars on my face, some knew my story - most didn't. No one asked what happened – but I probably wouldn't have volunteered the information anyhow. I'm not sure I ever told some of my best friends my whole story. If I didn't talk about it, then it didn't happen…. Right?

What no one knew was what I was feeling on the inside. They didn't see what was under the surface of the water – the large, deep, complicated portion of the iceberg. I was floundering, trying to stay above water with a smile on my face, acting like everything was okay - when, in fact, it wasn't.

How do you continue putting on a brave face day after day, when all you want to do is curl up and sleep? I was depressed, but I didn't recognize it at the time. I needed to talk to a professional who could help me navigate the world of trauma. The words "mental health" never came up in school, and we were never taught about the importance of it. When a subject is so taboo, who wants to bring it up?

***

Reflection

What was middle school like for you? What are your immediate thoughts when you think of it?

What was (or is) high school like for you? If you are still in high school, how do you envision the rest of your time there being like?

When you think of the words "mental health," what thoughts come to mind?

5

Life After 18

> **I didn't realize just how much the old trauma had affected my life and would continue to do so until I did something about it.**

I continued living the same life, day after day. It was my comfortable routine. Wake up, get ready, go to class. Go to dance or track practice. Perform at football or basketball games on the weekends. I loved routine. But high school was coming to an end, and I needed to figure out my next step.

I applied to college - but only in-state. I couldn't see myself leaving the comfort of my family. I was accepted to Colorado State University and accepted the offer because that was what everyone else was doing. Sure, I wanted to experience it, but now looking back, I wasn't ready – mentally or emotionally. In college I kept thinking things were going to be different, just like my first day of high school. I didn't realize just how much the old trauma had affected my life and would continue to do so until I did something about it.

It took me longer to mature than others my age. The trauma in my brain affected the frontal lobe, which is responsible for decision making skills, and damage to it can cause social and emotional changes. I did not recognize this and thought that my behaviors and social awkwardness were due to being "shy." I allowed myself to remain unaware of the deep impact that the crash had on my mental ability to process emotions.

College

As a freshman in college, I got lucky with the people in my dorm. My good friend from high school, Kelly, lived in the room next door to mine, and we shared a bathroom. I think she was my saving grace. She was outgoing, introducing me to people, bringing me along to parties with her and her new friends. We got along great with both of our roommates, and I slowly became comfortable with my new life.

Our floor had a big open area that had carpeted benches. It was a total eighties-era scene. The whole floor would sit out there with our blankets and pillows on Sundays watching football on TVs that the guys would bring out. We would also walk together to the gym across the street and encourage each other to workout. I got lucky. I found a good groove freshman year, but still felt that I wasn't being who I really was. I don't think I ever mentioned my car crash in college.

College is a time for exploration and trying to figure out where you want to go with your life. I finally decided to major in history because I wanted to be a teacher; my two favorite teachers in high school taught history and I wanted to make a difference in kids' lives, like they did in mine. Also, history was a lot of writing, which I loved. I was never good at those multiple-choice tests; I preferred to show my knowledge through my own words.

I didn't end up going into the teaching program because I was scared. I was scared that it was going to be too much work or I would fail, and I was afraid that I wouldn't be able to communicate clearly with students' parents had I become a teacher. I didn't want to deal with the conflicts that would arise with teaching. I felt that because I couldn't often communicate with my own friends, I would never be able to communicate with students that I was responsible for teaching.

A lot of what I experienced in college was relevant to how I felt about myself – low self-esteem, no confidence. I hung on to those people who wanted to be my friends, and didn't try hard to make new friends. I feel like I allowed people to come to me instead of putting myself out there.

Surprise

I got pregnant when I was 19. I have never been able to say exactly when it happened or who the father was. I have not fully processed this with my therapist, but I am planning on doing EMDR (eye movement desensitization and reprocessing) to help bring back my memories. It is one of the lowest moments of my life.

I found out I was pregnant because I was extremely sick. I was living in a sorority house at the time, and I was on the couch where we were all watching TV. I was lying on the lap of one of my sisters, and she said I was burning up and I had the chills. I told her I was fine and I went to bed. We had to move out the next day because our house was closing (that's a story for another time!). I moved all of my boxes and clothes by myself because I refused to ask for help. A few days later, I was still feverish, so I went to the on-campus doctor.

Immediately after doing a physical exam she had me take a pregnancy test. It came back positive. I was mortified. She sat there and made me call someone to tell them. I called my brother Ryan, who is in the Navy, and I knew he was out at sea at that time. I left a voicemail and that seemed to placate the doctor. She told me I needed to get to a hospital. I told her I would and walked home.

I tried to make it through one more night. I called my dad the next morning and told him I was very sick. He dropped everything and came to pick me up. At the urgent care, I found out I had a kidney infection. I had been moved to a bed in urgent care so the nurses could give me fluids. They were going to transfer me to the hospital, but before that happened, the nurse asked if my parents knew I was pregnant. I told her they didn't.

My parents came in the room and sat on the sides of the hospital bed I was in. In the extremely awkward silence, I looked at the nurse and nodded. I couldn't say it and luckily the nurse understood and she gave my parents the news. There were tears in their eyes, and I felt their confusion as to why I would hide this, but they said they would support me 100%. I knew they would – they were always there for me.

I spent a few days in the hospital, and once I recovered, I went back to school. I hid my pregnancy. Or at least I tried. I wore large sweatshirts once I started showing. I worked out for hours a day. I took my prenatal vitamins because I didn't want to get sick again and because I knew that was the right thing to do. I didn't know what to do - I just wanted my life to get back to normal and not be judged by my situation.

> **This pregnancy wasn't going away and I had to figure out what I was going to do.**

I was in my bedroom at my parent's house when I decided to call an adoption agency. Now, at this time I was lucky if I could get the courage to call and order pizza, so this was a big step for me. I made an appointment to talk to a counselor. She could see me right away, so I got in my car and drove to her office.

I had to sit in the car for a while and force myself to go in. This pregnancy wasn't going away and I had to figure out what I was going to do. I went into the office. The lighting was low and calming. Kate, the counselor, was very kind. I filled out some paperwork, and we just talked. It was the first time I had felt comfortable talking openly about being pregnant. I didn't talk to anyone else outside of that office about my feelings.

I was given profiles of people who were waiting to adopt a child. Do you know how hard it is to be the one to decide who will get a child? It was one of the hardest decisions of my life. I knew I couldn't give the child the life they deserved, and I wanted to help someone else. Once I made my decision, I felt at peace. I met the family and knew it was the right choice. They were amazing people.

I continued to hide the pregnancy, or so I thought. My friends Mary and Kelly came over one night and told me they knew. I tried to deny it, but it was no use. My roommates also knew, and they were extremely supportive. Even though I didn't want to talk about it, they were still there for me. I truly don't know how I would have made it through this without Jess, Kara, and Kristin.

I would get random phone calls from people who would ask if the rumors were true. Was I really pregnant? Who was the father? I kept shutting them down, blatantly lying because I was scared out of my mind. And then there were the people who assumed they knew more about what I should do than I did myself. It was a flood of emotions, and it was no wonder why I kept retreating back into my own world, only leaving home for class and the grocery store.

I regularly drove home to go to doctor visits. When it was time to go to the hospital for an induction, I left my house and remember my roommate Jess giving me a card that said to be strong, and that she admired me for what I was doing. I cried the whole hour's drive to my parents house. I let Kate, the counselor, know that I was headed in to the hospital. It was a fast labor. I don't remember much of it but I was glad it was over. I didn't want to hold the baby, but let the real parents be the first to cuddle their bundle of joy.

***

After I left the hospital and was back home with my roommates, I continued living my life like nothing happened. I got comments about how skinny I was, and how people had missed seeing me out. It was some of the hardest months of my life, and once again, I found myself losing a lot of friendships because I had secluded myself for so many months. I had also lost a lot of friendships from high school by this time. Those people who I thought would be in my life forever were no longer there. I had abandoned them, and they had abandoned me.

I was suffering from postpartum depression. While I was able to put on that brave face, like I did after my car crash, I still knew something wasn't right. I yearned for love and attention from others. I saw an article in the college newspaper about the health center, and I ended up seeing an on-campus therapist. I don't know what made me do it, but much like the call that I made to the adoption center, it was a very tough call to make.

I only had a few sessions. I didn't feel like we discussed anything extremely deep, but then again, the trauma of this time affected my memory. This opened the door for me, though, into the world of therapy. I started to see the benefits of talking to a third party about what was happening in my life. A non-judgmental person who can listen and help me talk myself through it. A seed was planted and I would continue to mull over the thought of going back to therapy for the next few years.

※ ※ ※

Reflection

What have you experienced in your life that you have hid from others?

Why did you hide it? What fear did/do you have if someone found out about your secret?

Do you still carry this around, or have you shared it with someone else? If you are still carrying your secret, what impact is it having on your life?

6

Getting Help

Between the time of my first college therapy session (around 2006) and when I went to my next one in 2018, my life was a roller coaster. Yearning for love and attention, I went from relationship to relationship and, after I turned 21, spent a lot of time at the bars. I decided to get a second job when a new restaurant was opening in town. It was here that I met my now ex-husband. We hastily got into a relationship that was unhealthy when I was 23. We got married two years later and quickly had a beautiful baby boy.

The relationship didn't start out strong, but we were young and having fun. He drank a lot; we argued a lot. I stopped drinking when I was pregnant and started to realize that our relationship had focused around drinking. I also thought that a baby would fix everything. The marriage was a slow and steady downhill slide that I hid the from my family and friends. I did not know at the time that what I was going though was not okay (which, for many reasons, I won't detail in this book).

Finding Positivity

One day, my sister-in-law invited me to a party where she was a consultant for a direct selling company. I took a leap of faith that day and joined this company because it would help her out with her sales and I would get a discount on products. This ended up being the life changing moment I needed.

> **I had never had that feeling of camaraderie and friendship with a group.**

I went to weekly meetings that were full of positive messages, real friendships without judgment, and genuine fun. We worked on ourselves – figuring out our limiting beliefs, how to overcome them, and how to reach our goals. I started to look forward to Tuesday nights - a much needed girls night that I hadn't had in years.

I had never had that feeling of camaraderie and friendship with a group. It was at these meetings that I found my voice and started to speak up and share some of my fears. I also started to learn that many women shared the same fears - the fear of judgment, the fear of loss, the fear of change.

IOME

It was within this group of women that I met Becky, the woman who would help me change my life. I began therapy at the beginning of 2018, as part of a pilot project with a company Becky started called IOME. Becky wanted women to start caring for themselves first, an "I owe me" instead of an "I owe you." She doesn't want individuals to live life day after day, feeling stuck. She wants us to thrive!

I don't know what made me say yes to being a part of the pilot program, but I did. I was putting myself out there, which was something I had never done. *Self care* - what was that? We sat down and did an assessment of my goals, my fears and my setbacks, and then made a plan to start working on those areas.

I was so nervous when I walked in the office for my first therapy appointment. Was I really doing this? Should I do this? The room was filled with light, bright colors, with a beautiful backdrop of the town square. The first few sessions were really about getting to know me. I had never talked so much about myself before.

I started talking with Becky about my life and where I wanted to go, and what was holding me back. She guided me with questions; her expertise knowing what to ask and when to probe deeper. She also encouraged me to take time for myself - go to a yoga class, read a book, take a bubble bath. The simple things in life that could help my mindset and allow me to be a better mom, friend, daughter, sister.

I slowly realized that I could be in control of my life. I realized that my thoughts and feelings were genuine and needed to be heard. I realized that I had been through multiple extraordinary traumas (the car crash, the pregnancy, the marriage) and that they had affected my life tremendously since 1997. I also realized that it was time to get a divorce, for my mental health, and for the benefit my son's future.

Through IOME and therapy, I realized that I could use my experience to help others. I reached out to MADD (Mother's Against Drunk Driving) to see if I could be a volunteer. I was contacted by an amazing woman who asked if I ever thought about telling my story. I truly never thought that speaking in public would be something I would ever do past college. However, something made me say yes.

My first time speaking at a Victim Impact Panel, I was a mess. I was so nervous. I had my note cards in front of me, typed out and ready. Becky came with me for support. As I looked out into the crowd of people who had been convicted of drinking and driving, I realized that by telling my story I was helping to keep Aunt Julie's spirit alive, as well as the spirit of the AirLife Crew who died in the crash - Pete, Beth, and Leslie. If my story can help someone to not drink and drive, then a life could be saved, heartache and trauma could be prevented.

> **My main goal is to help others realize that their actions can affect others lives in unimaginable ways.**

I have now been speaking at MADD for three years and counting, and each time I feel a sense of hope. I have told my story in classrooms and assemblies, and also at conferences and events. I always wonder where I would be had I not joined that company, had I not met Becky, and had she not started IOME.

My main goal is to help others realize that their actions can affect others lives in unimaginable ways. A man I didn't know, and will never know, decided to drink and drive and have an impact on my entire life. From the bullying I endured, to the helplessness I felt, to being stuck in my 12-year-old mind, that all could have been prevented. I have realized that life is all about choices, and am glad I have now chosen to use my past to help others.

* * *

Therapy changed my life. Not only was I learning how to be emotionally stable, but I was also processing events that I didn't know I needed to process. I realized that my life is worth something. It was the help I didn't know I needed.

Not all trauma looks like mine. Trauma does not have to be a car accident or physical damage to your body. Trauma is defined as a response to an event that someone finds highly stressful. There are many types of trauma - bullying, harassment, physical or sexual assault, witnessing an accident or terrible event, community violence such as school shootings, domestic abuse, racism, traffic accidents, natural disasters, losing someone close, unwanted pregnancy. The list can go on and on.

It takes a lot of mental strength to acknowledge your trauma and seek help. But to move past the trauma, to grow from it and learn from it, that first step must be taken. It's okay to be selfish and put your mental health before everything else. You must continuously work on improving yourself. There will be setbacks, but you can gain the knowledge and ability to push through those setbacks with a little guidance.

Therapy changed my life.

* * *

Reflection

Write down a time when you had to leave your comfort zone. What were the feelings you had? How did you convince yourself to do something you really didn't want to do?

Who is one person in your life who has helped you through a tough time? Have you told them what an impact they had on you?

Have you experienced a trauma? What about an experience that you didn't think was a trauma, but has continued to have an impact on your life?

II

Part Two

"The best way out is always through." - Robert Frost

7

Let's Talk Therapy and Mental Health

I am now a single mother, in a loving relationship, raising my son to be well rounded and mentally healthy. I still have a lot of struggles. I still have social issues and days when I feel very down. I still feel judged by others. There are days when I don't feel good enough and when I can't motivate myself to do the daily tasks. The struggle does not end once you acknowledge your traumas, but you will be better at dealing with your feelings and emotions once you take that leap.

As adults, we want our children to be equipped with the tools to grow into healthy adults. However, adults will have a hard time raising mentally healthy children if they themselves are struggling with traumas and mental health issues. The subject of mental health has become more mainstream in the past few years, but it still carries a stigma.

"You're crazy."

"Are you dangerous?"

"Are you going to kill yourself?"

"You're different."

People aren't likely to say these things to your face, but rather, talk about you behind your back. The social and public perception of being depressed or suffering from a mental illness is what keeps people from seeking help. If people were to know that you were depressed, do you think they would treat you differently? In a good or bad way? Do you think they would respect you for telling them, or not know how to act around you?

> **The social and public perception of being depressed or suffering from a mental illness is what keeps people from seeking help.**

What if they respected your decision for telling them, and then asked questions about it? Maybe they themselves are depressed and have not told anyone about their feelings, until you came out about it. How would that change your relationship? If you had an open conversation with your spouse, best friend, parents, or kids about your feelings, do you think they would alienate you or embrace you?

I have struggled on and off with depression. When I was younger, I had no idea that my feelings of being sad, lonely, and misunderstood were connected to my depression. For so long I had struggled with just trying to get back to who I was before the crash that I didn't take the time to confront my mental health. I pretended to be someone I wasn't - to the detriment of myself and those around me.

The more mental health is discussed openly, the more people will talk about it; the more people talk about it, the more people will be helped. I have so much respect for people who are willing to talk about their experience with therapy, trauma, depression, anxiety, eating disorders, being bi-polar, PTSD. It is not easy to start these conversations. It is not easy to ask for help. But it is the way to start living a life that is freer than the one you are living when stuck in the cage of a mental health illness.

Therapy Isn't Scary

How do you deal with the fear you get deep in the pit of your stomach when you think of talking about your trauma? I am very familiar with that feeling. For me, it is like the feeling of jumping out of an airplane. You're dizzy, you can't help looking down, your stomach is in knots but at the same time it's flipping like crazy. You break out in a sweat. You get hot and then cold. You don't want people to know about how you are feeling because you are afraid of being judged.

One day, you find an ounce of braveness in your heart and act on it before it goes away. You take one small step. That step can be looking up a therapist's phone number or asking a school counselor or your doctor for a referral. The next step might be driving to your appointment or stepping into the office.

Another small step will be getting past the formalities of the initial meeting with the therapist. The fear might still be there. You might be worried about how you will be judged in the room you are sitting in. You might be worried about what will happen if you speak about something that you have never talked about.

Then you open your mouth. You tell your therapist about your past. It starts to get easier to talk about. You dive into the depths of your mind and learn more about yourself than you ever knew before. You start to analyze why you think and act the way you do. You start to see your trauma differently - instead of seeing trauma as something that is holding you down, you begin to see it as something that can push you up.

My Experience

> **One after the other, the memories were untangling and becoming a clear picture - a picture I had never seen before.**

When I processed my car crash, Becky used EMDR* therapy – eye movement desensitization and reprocessing. To put it simply, EMDR helps retrieve memories that the brain is hiding. First, Becky and I established my "safe place." This is place I can go to in my head if the memories got too intense. I was then given buzzers in each hand that lightly buzzed in a pattern. After taking deep breaths, Becky asked me to go back to a specific moment that we had previously talked about. Once in this moment, I let my mind go. I started to verbalize the pictures in my mind. One after the other, the memories were untangling and becoming a clear picture - a picture I had never seen before.

Becky and I then unpacked the memories, and, over time, I was able to start "seeing" more of the crash. I was able to see the headlights coming toward us. My Aunt Julie on the steering wheel. The firefighter standing over me. Me waking up in the ICU. At times, it almost felt like I was making up these stories. But from the little details I had heard and read about the crash, I knew that these were the full memories that had been hidden from me.

As an outsider looking in, it was an incredible experience to unlock these memories. For me, it was exhausting, yet worth every second. While processing these memories, I started to see how dramatically this incident changed my life. I was able to understand how I hid the traumatic events from my conscious mind. Avoiding the memories was my brain's way of protecting me.

I also saw that I was holding on to my past so hard that I wasn't allowing myself to grow or allowing myself to grieve. I always thought that I was just a victim of someone's decision. I didn't realize how stuck I was; I was trying to grow up while a part of my mind was still wishing I could go back to December 14th and tell my Aunt Julie I didn't want to see the Nutcracker.

It took me a long time to face what happened. It might take you a long time to get over your fear of talking or the fear of stigmas involved with seeing a therapist. Once you start, it might take a while to get to the root of the issue. Therapy can be (and should be) a lifelong journey, much like when you go to your family physician for a checkup. There will be seasons when you need a lot of therapy, and seasons where an occasional check-in is all that is needed.

I'll put references in the back of the book so you can read more about EMDR and other types of therapy. I am not an expert, so I don't want to get something wrong here!

Just Try It

I feel a question coming on... what if I can't afford therapy?

Think about it as an investment into your future. It is not as expensive as you think, and there are plenty of resources and assistance you can find. Some health insurance plans cover it, and some employers have an employee assistance plan that includes therapy. Nowadays, you don't even have to leave the comfort of your home to have a virtual appointment.

Whether you try therapy or not, it is important to have people in your life who you can communicate with about what is going on in your world. If you don't have family or friends that are willing to understand what you are going through, there are many options to find people you connect with. Small groups, churches, and online clubs are a good place to start. There are many people who are going through what you are - you just need to be willing to do the work to find them.

I used to (and still do) get stuck in a pattern of thinking of "I don't know what to do or who to reach out to on this issue, so I am just going to do nothing." And then I am stuck. It takes me a while to get out of being stuck and realizing that I am the only one that can help myself. I need to take the next step to be the person I know I can be. The person who I am supposed to be. The person I was made to be.

> **It takes me a while to get out of being stuck and realizing that I am the only one that can help myself.**

* * *

When fear tries to take over, you need to realize that you are the only one who can be accountable for yourself. You are accountable for your actions and your reactions. Remembering this has helped me take small steps in the right direction, especially on days when I am paralyzed by fear. Working through my traumas and realizing that I am the only person responsible for my happiness has helped me to move out of the feeling of being stuck in my 12-year-old self.

After you acknowledge the trauma, it is important to remain accountable to yourself. This can be more demanding than you think. You will have bad days. You might regress. Therapy is not a cure all, but rather a way to talk about how your past is affecting your present and allow yourself to move into a positive, healthy future.

* * *

Reflection

What stigma do you have when you hear the word "therapy?"

When is a time you have been stuck in a negative pattern of thinking? What did you do, or can you do in the future, to get out of that head space and into a more positive one?

8

Are You a Bully?

Do you want to know what is scary? Writing out some of your deepest thoughts and feelings and publishing it. I have put off writing this book and publishing my thoughts in my blog because of the intense hate that can come through the internet. I was afraid of those people who I grew up with finally learning how scared I was as a child. I was afraid of those friends I lost in college because I tried to hide a pregnancy and didn't open up to them. No one realized how devastating that time was for me – because I didn't tell anyone how I was feeling.

I am afraid of putting something online that fuels someone to say hateful things. I know this book isn't going to be perfect. Too long, too short, grammatical errors, confusing, hard to follow. Probably some of the many comments that people will make. It's funny to me how a book that talks about being judged and bullying will be judged by its readers. Oh well. I am putting this out there to help just one person realize that they are not alone. If I touch one person's life, it will be a success.

> **No one realized how devastating that time was for me – because I didn't tell anyone how I was feeling.**

I decided to write this book because I finally realized that what I have been through is not unique. Others have trauma, have been bullied, have lost friends, and have kept secrets. If I have a notion about sharing an idea, that idea did not come by chance. It was put there because that is what my purpose is. My purpose is to share, and if I can help one person become stronger about their past, or seek therapy, or overcome a fear, or stop drinking and driving, then I have succeeded.

Remember how I was supposed to be in that helicopter? Now I am here sharing a story that I have kept in my heart for over 20 years.

The Iceberg

What have you put off because of the fear of judgment or bullying by others? When a person is bullying or judging someone else, they have no idea what might be going on in that person's life. You see one side of people - the side they want you to see. There is a whole world going on underneath your perceptions.

I talked of an iceberg earlier, and how I felt that no one really knew what was happening with me. Now, I want you all to picture an iceberg. You can see the top, but you can't see what is underneath by looking at the surface. You can't see how deep the iceberg goes or how complicated it is underneath the surface. There are crevices that will never see the light above the surface.

I want you to think of this iceberg as a person – their face and body are above the surface - what you see. Their heart, mind and thoughts are what you cannot see. You can assume many things, such as what they are thinking, what they went though in an experience, how they feel. The truth is, you will never know what is really under the surface.

If you could see what was beneath the surface, would you act differently toward that person?

Put yourself in the shoes of someone who is bullying another person. What do you think could be going on in the bully's life that is contributing to their behavior? While there is no need to justify their words or actions, it is possible that the kid (or adult) who is bullying has been taught from a young age that yelling, name calling, and being aggressive toward someone else is normal. It is also believed that people who are judgmental or who bully others are projecting their own beliefs about themselves onto their victims.

Now put yourself in the shoes of someone who is being bullied. Again, you can only see the surface. You have no idea what they might be facing in their life - a crisis at home, a death in the family, a lack of food or necessities, emotional or physical abuse, low self-esteem. If you could see what was beneath the surface, would you act differently toward that person?

The kids at school knew I had been in a car crash. However, they did not know the extent of the damage that it caused mentally. At the time, I did not realize the extent of the damage either. I had been on the receiving end of another person's bad decision. I had seen my Aunt pass away next to me. I had daily headaches. I had to go through physical therapy and wait for my scars to heal, which took years. They are still visible today. I had a deep belief that it was my fault that the crash happened; after all, I was a dancer, I wanted to see the Nutcracker, I didn't press the issue of the broken seat belt for Aunt Julie.

Would she still be alive if she were wearing it?

The kids at school, who made fun of my scars, didn't know what I was going through. They didn't know that every time they opened their mouths about the scars on my face, it reminded me that I believed the crash was my fault. It reminded me of Aunt Julie. It reminded me that she wasn't with us anymore. The kids had no idea of the trauma I had been through, and if they knew, would they have used kinder words?

Adult Bullies

Kids are not the only bullies out there. Adults can be so cruel to each other. Look at any online post where someone writes something that others disagree with. People get into verbal arguments, name calling, putting each other down, and being hateful, hurtful human beings. For being the "Land of the Free," some adults certainly have an issue with others who have a different opinion than them.

It is the adults who are the role models for our children. Children aren't born to bully. They have learned it somewhere along the way. Maybe from parents, older siblings, cousins, teachers, preachers, coaches - what are you saying in front of your children, or the children you are around, that is shaping them into who they are growing up to be?

Do you have a teacher or coach that you spend/spent a lot of time with who is consistently negative and put others down? Does your child have a cousin or older friend who has questionable beliefs and morals that go against how you live? Do you verbally assault others or emotionally abuse people? Your kids model the behavior they see and take that into adulthood.

In my life, I see adults being cruel to each other in unimaginable ways, in front of kids - sometimes at youth sports games in front of an entire audience. When I see adults acting cruel, I always think about how they are raising their kids and what their home life is like. Are they perpetuating the cycle of bullying?

Are they the parents of the kids who bullied another kid to the point of suicide?

Are they ignorant because of the way they were raised, or are they bullying to make a sick point about leadership (bullying to get what you want) and being assertive?

Likely the adult does not think of their behavior as "bullying," and if no one stops them, it will continue.

We need to make a change. We can't keep treating other adults with such hate, because, whether you are a parent or not, it is kids who see this and think the cruel behavior is acceptable. Ask yourself this - do you think bullying is acceptable behavior? How are you raising your children, or plan to raise them in the future, to stop the cycle of bullying?

Watch Your Words

A few months after my car crash, my dad enrolled in a citizen's police academy. In one session, the class was talking about DUI's, and my crash was being used as an example. My dad left the room, telling the officer who led the class that he wasn't ready to see these pictures and explained why. A few minutes later, a man who overheard the conversation came up to my dad and told him, "that crash happened a while ago. You should get over it."

Get over it? No one is allowed to tell you when you are done healing. **Ever.**

The man who said that had no right to say those words, but I often wonder what trauma he might be dealing with that he needs to face. What is under the surface of the water that made him act like that?

What is under your surface that you need to come to terms with?

***

Reflection

Have you ever walked up to a group of people and immediately knew they were talking about you? How did you feel?

Have you been talking badly about a friend of yours and that friend walked up? How did you feel?

Have you ever been uncomfortable speaking up because you are worried someone is going to judge you?

Do you ever agree with something you are uncomfortable with just because "everyone else is doing it?"

Are you taking care of your mental health right now? How?

9

Self Care

I take care of myself first. My well being, my mental health, my physical health. I have done the work, and continue to do the work, to find those crevices beneath the surface that I need to work on. I found that this is the only way I can be sure that I am taking care of everyone else in my life. Have you heard the saying, "You can't pour out of an empty cup?" You can't pour your love into anyone else if you do not love yourself first.

I'm sure you have had a day where you woke up "on the wrong side of the bed." You feel that everything and everyone is agitating you. Every little situation gets under your skin, but you can't pinpoint the reason. I have had a lot of days like that. Everyone has. A few days ago, my son had the case to his earbuds in his hand and kept snapping the lid shut. Open, shut. Open, shut. I noticed he was doing it, but it didn't bother me.

The next day, we were driving, and it was open, shut. Open, shut. Open, shut. I asked him to stop, and he didn't. I snapped at him to stop. He looked at me surprised and put the case down. I don't usually snap. I should have asked him again, maybe firmer this time, to stop. I shouldn't have snapped. What changed?

The noise didn't change. I did.

> **SELF CARE. Embrace it. Love it. Get to know it. You - and the people in your life - will thank you for having these two little words in your vocabulary.**

It has taken me a while, but I can now recognize when my cup is empty. When I can't do the things I usually do with the same vigor or when I start being cranky toward everyone in my path, I know I need to take a step back to recharge my batteries. I need to fill up that cup again. The only way I can stop the negativity in my head is to take a big step back and reflect on how I have been treating myself.

SELF CARE. Embrace it. Love it. Get to know it. You - and the people in your life - will thank you for having these two little words in your vocabulary.

How you are treating others reflects how you feel about yourself. Let's go back to me snapping at my son. He does not deserve to be snapped at, especially if the day prior, I was allowing him to make that noise and did not correct him. If I go back and think about the day, I was irritated that my car had failed its emissions. I was going to have to bring it to the dealership and pay to find out what was wrong, and then pay again to have it fixed (it ended up being a recall, but I didn't know that at the time)!

It was a late night because we were going from school, to a quick dinner at my parents', to a football practice that was going to go late. I wouldn't be home until 8:00 pm, making it a 12+ hour day. I was running on fumes and had eaten coffee and a pastry for breakfast, Taco Bell for lunch, and then tacos again for dinner - and probably an energy drink or two in between.

I did not feel good about myself on this day. I had overeaten in the junk food category. I thought I was going to have to shell out money to fix my car. I hadn't prepared for the long day ahead. I hadn't had enough water, either. My brain was foggy, and I was just trying to make it from one activity to the next. Does any of this sound familiar?

I was not treating myself like I deserve. I was taking shortcuts (fast food for lunch and dinner) and not being smart with my water intake. I know better! I try to preach to my son about drinking water and trying to make healthy choices, and I failed to listen to my own advice. I was feeling down about myself, and I took those feelings and made my son feel like he was doing something wrong. He was just being a 10-year-old.

I needed to improve how I was treating myself.

Make It About You

I want you to think about one thing in your life that you want to improve. It must be about you, no one else. Do you want to drink more water? Sleep more? Become more active? Find a new career? Face a past trauma? Be nicer to your significant other, or to yourself?

Once you think of what you want to improve, write down five things you can do right now to improve that. Can't think of anything? Google "how to _____". I just searched for "how to drink more water" and right at the top is a list of 12 ways to do it.

Next, get to work! Dig out that old water bottle or your favorite pair of tennis shoes. Send a loving text message to someone you've been needing to reach out to. Look for therapists in your area. Plan to do one small thing each day to improve.

Taking care of yourself can be different for different people. People, especially women, are inherently inclined to want to take care of others first. Here are some things that you can do right now for a little self-care.

- Go for a walk
- Read a book
- Journal
- Drink some tea
- Write 10 things you are grateful for
- Say a prayer
- Take a nap
- Do something crafty
- Have a dance party
- Stretch
- De-clutter a spot in the house
- Paint
- Sleep in
- Bake
- Get a massage
- Say no
- Go for a walk
- Meditate

If you start living life in a way that is respectful of yourself, you will start to see improvements in other areas of life. You will start to show those around you that self-care is a part of the journey of life! I don't care what gender you are, what you look like, how much money you have or don't have, every one of us needs to take care of ourselves before we are able to take care of others.

You might not agree, and you'll come up with excuses. Netflix is not an excuse. Laundry is not an excuse. "Can't afford therapy" is not an excuse. Poor time management is not an excuse. Having homework or studying is not an excuse. There is no excuse to not care for your own well being. There are always opportunities for you to grow; you need to want the changes you seek bad enough to go after them.

Looking back on my life and my decisions, I was treating myself poorly for a very long time. I was also letting others treat me poorly, mainly because I thought that was what I deserved. My self-esteem was low, and I would take any "love" I thought I could get.

I spent the majority of my twenties in a tailspin of trying to figure out life with a partner who didn't make me happy, trying to raise a child seemingly on my own, trying to run from my past, and not facing life head on. I was so blessed and lucky that my thirties took a turn. I can't imagine where my life would be had I not gone to therapy and learned the value of caring for myself.

Taking care of yourself is not just facing past traumas. It is not just going to therapy or a small group. It is not just talking to your friends about what is going on in your life. It can be all of the above or none of the above. Self-care is doing what makes you the happiest and healthiest individual you can be.

While therapy was my first step, it doesn't have to be for everyone. I had a deep trauma that needed to be sorted out in my brain. The car crash was my source of pain for many, many years. Talking through it made me aware of the impact it had on me, and I felt an intense amount of freedom once I made that realization.

Continuous Struggles

I continue to work on myself each day. I am far from perfect, and I never will be perfect. We all have our flaws and missteps. I still have anxiety when I am around groups of people, even if I know them. I do better with one-on-one situations. I am working on my group anxiety and it has gotten a lot better over the years. I prefer to sit back and listen to the conversation. I am never the center of attention, and that's okay. I am perfectly content with awkward silences and quiet car rides.

> **There are days when my hair is a mess, my house is a mess, and I feel like my life is a mess.**

I struggle with motivation. I like to put tasks off until the last minute because I think that I work better under pressure. What happens then, of course, is that I need to get a lot of work done in a small amount of time, adding unnecessary stress. I have tried countless "systems" that people say work for them. It wasn't until I realized that I am my own, unique person and what works for one person is not always going to work for me. Through trial and error, I have found that having an accountability partner is the best thing for my motivation and getting projects done.

I struggle with self esteem and have days where I think everyone is judging me. There are days when my hair is a mess, my house is a mess, and I feel like my life is a mess. I know everyone has these days, but society tells us that we need to keep those messy things to ourselves. Social media tells us to envy what others have and judge yourself based the "perfect life" other people are posting.

How will we improve our lives if we take the scary things and hide them under the bed? How would your life change if you talked to someone about the scary things?

We will always have something to work on and work towards. The dilemma comes when we realize how much work it will be, how scary the work can be, and how long it will take. Trust me, though, the freedom you feel when you can face your fears, face your past, and put it behind you, is worth it.

YOU ARE WORTH IT!

* * *

SELF CARE

Reflection

What will you do, today, for yourself?

How can you make self care a permanent part of your lifestyle?

10

Thank You

If you've gotten this far, thank you. Thank you for reading my story and becoming invested in my life. This wasn't easy for me, and the butterflies I have in my stomach are going crazy just thinking about people reading through my past, but for me, it was a necessary step in my healing.

If you get just one thing from reading my story, let it be this:

<u>Your actions and your words have a great impact on others.</u>

This can be for good or for bad. Remember this as you live your life.

Don't get behind the wheel after drinking.

Don't judge others for things you can't understand.

Acknowledge your own traumas.

Take care of your mental health.

Don't be a bully.

THANK YOU

Be kind, not only to others but to yourself.

Ask for help.

Be who you are, not who you think others want you to be.

If you feel inclined, share your story with someone. You never know whose lives you might touch if you do. We have all been through something, and knowing we are not alone in our traumas can bring a lot of healing to our world.

11

Resources

Here are a few of the resources I mentioned. Check them out below!

IOME:
www.iowemenow.com

EMDR Therapy:
www.emdria.org

Types of Therapy:
www.psychologytoday.com/us/types-of-therapy

Mother's Against Drunk Driving:
www.madd.org

Substance Abuse and Mental Health Hotline:
1-800-662-4357

Anti-Bullying:
www.stopbullying.gov

Therapy for Every Budget

RESOURCES

https://www.healthline.com/health/therapy-for-every-budget

* * *

In the following pages, there are pictures of the crash that may be triggering for some individuals.

12

A Picture is Worth 1000 Words

I struggled to determine if I should put these pictures in this book or not. I decided to because pictures are worth more than words, and the visuals below help tell my story. All of the pictures of the car and me in the hospital were taken by my parents, who bravely documented what had happened.

The pictures of my Aunt Julie were sent to me by my cousin Lizzy, and I am grateful that we have them. I wish I had a picture of me and Aunt Julie the night we went out for our final adventure. She was a beautiful soul, an amazing human being, and she will always live on in our memory.

A PICTURE IS WORTH 1000 WORDS

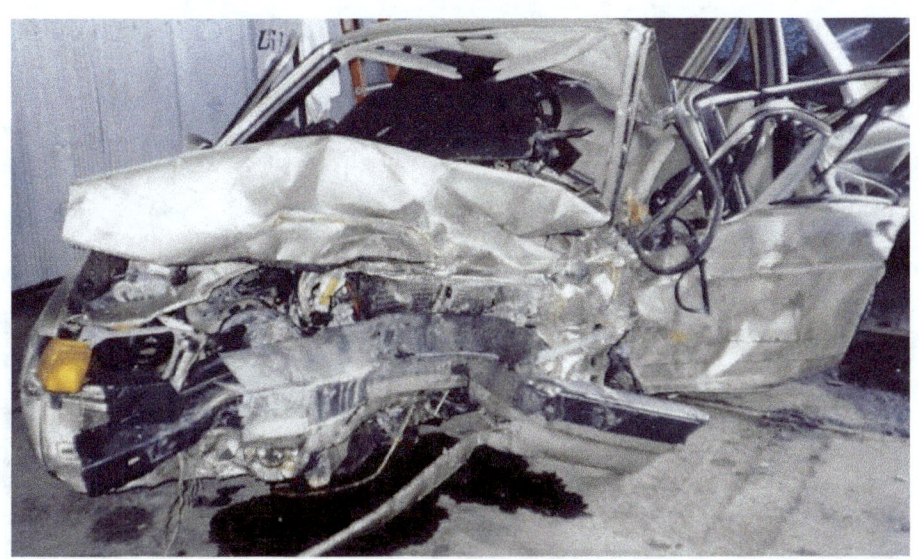

My Aunt Julie's car

Where I was sitting

A PICTURE IS WORTH 1000 WORDS

The car that caused the crash, with my Aunt Julie's car in the background

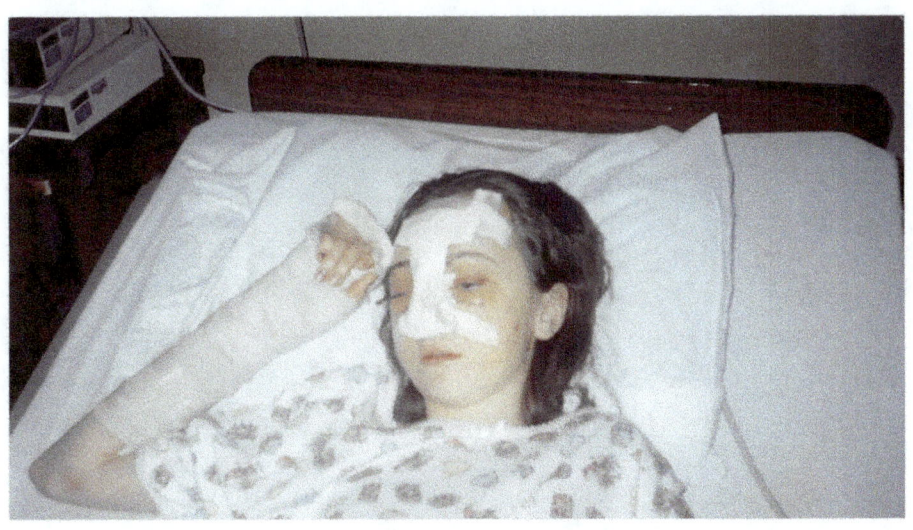

Post-surgery

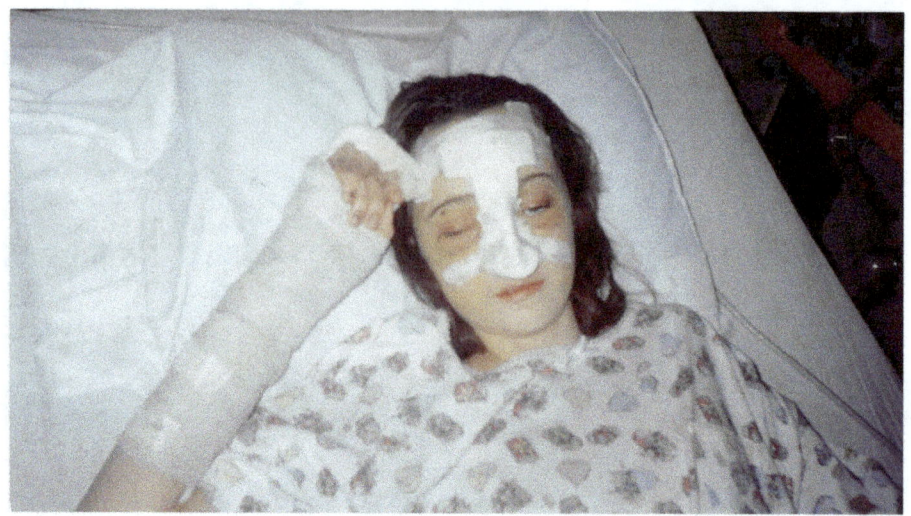

Post Surgery

Me, my little sister Kristin and my cousin Lizzy

My Uncle Jay, Aunt Julie, and Uncle Johnny (late 80's)

Aunt Julie with my cousin Lizzy, me, my brother Ryan, and my cousin Zack (early 90's)

A PICTURE IS WORTH 1000 WORDS

Happy, healthy, FREE.

About the Author

Brittany Lamb was born and raised in the beautiful state of Colorado. Her family and close friends are the most important aspect of her life. She is passionate about helping others see how the past does not have to dictate your future. Brittany wants every individual to know you are your own best advocate. No one can change you except for you! You can find more of her writing on her website, www.thinkfiftytwenty.com

You can connect with me on:
- https://www.thinkfiftytwenty.com
- https://www.facebook.com/thinkfiftytwenty
- https://www.instagram.com/brittanymarielamb

www.ingramcontent.com/pod-product-compliance
Lightning Source LLC
LaVergne TN
LVHW021714080426
835510LV00010B/1002